Fuel and Camden People's Theatre present

SO MANY REASONS

Written and performed by Racheal Ofori

Directed by Zoe Lafferty

T0347998

Racheal Ofori

SO MANY REASONS

OBERON BOOKS
LONDON

WWW.OBERONBOOKS.COM

First published in 2020 by Oberon Books Ltd
521 Caledonian Road, London N7 9RH
Tel: +44 (0) 20 7607 3637 / Fax: +44 (0) 20 7607 3629
e-mail: info@oberonbooks.com
www.oberonbooks.com

A catalogue record for this book is available from the British Library.

PB ISBN: 9781786828538
E ISBN: 9781786828521

Cover image: Dan Tsantilis

Visit www.oberonbooks.com to read more about all our books and to buy them. You will
also find features, author interviews and news of any author events, and you can sign up for
e-newsletters and be the first to hear about our new releases.

PRAYER THERAPY

MEL enters. She gets down on her knees and puts her hands together.

Dear God. It's Melissa here.

I literally can't do this anymore…

I mean I'm not suicidal, but life is like so long…wow. Probably not for you because you exist outside of time blah blah whatever…but I'm only twenty-five.

Like sometimes, I just want a break from life. Like where you're not you. Is that a thing? Because technically I didn't ask to be here, on this journey, in this vehicle… (I mean it's quite an attractive vehicle, so thank you; things could be worse.) But the point is I didn't ask to be here so I should be able to tap out whenever I want you know?

Not death…because I haven't decided how I feel about you. I'm just asking for a little pause; a hiatus if you will. So can it commence now, and finish when things in my life are kind of completely, pretty much, entirely perfect. Thanks.

So, whenever you're ready… Woah! Not permanently! Just to be clear… Maybe we should have a safe word, like when I'm done being on a break…actually you don't need that – you're all-knowing, obviously.

Okay, cool. Go.

Silence. A sense that she might ascend and float to the heavens… but no – nothing.

Right, I'm getting vibes that this whole life hiatus thing… is not a thing. I thought it was worth a try but, cool, there's no get-out clause. And I think you missed a trick there – because we would probably all be better people if every now and then we could put a pause on life, and get a little objective perspective.

I just feel so lost. And I don't know where things went wrong…

THE BUCKET

I remember when I first visited Ghana.

I was ten and I was desperate to prove myself; show I was strong, I was clever, that I could learn the language.

Anyway where my grandma lives, when you're going to have a shower, you have to get a bucket and fill it up at the tap that serves the whole compound. The tap sits eclipsed by the shadow of a huge mango tree opposite. (And that mango tree is the bomb; never tasted mangos like it.)

The tap is next to where one of the uncles (that also lives in the compound) has set up his office. And when it's really hot his male colleagues will put a table outside in the shadow of the glorious mango tree and work there. Just near the tap.

So I stroll up with metal bucket in hand, ready for a shower – and I place it under the tap. And I see one of these male colleagues. Let's call him Uncle Eric. Oh, every elder is an 'uncle' or 'aunty', that's just how it works.

> **ERIC:** Do you want me to help you to carry that water?
>
> **MEL:** No. I can do it on my own.
>
> **ERIC:** Okay, okay, calm down British girl. I was only trying to help you.
>
> **MEL:** Help me where? To the shower??

And then he stands over me and watches me while the bucket fills.

> ERIC: Are you sure? It's going to be heavy.

ERIC chuckles.

And I look at him. And I laugh.

So I'm thinking I don't want the bucket to be too full so some of the water spills, giving him a reason to swoop in and save me and chaperone me to the shower. So I fill it just over halfway. And walk away. It's heavy but I do my best not to show it.

> ERIC: Oh! You are strong, oh. Wow. Strong
>   woman.

And I just laugh. I just laugh

And I still laugh now. Just to be nice.

It's interesting, though, because you end up with less water in your bucket...

THREE STRIPES

A crying young MEL comes home from school and throws her jacket down in front of her MUM.

> MEL: Mum, everyone laughed at me!

> MUM: What is wrong with you?

> MEL: Everyone laughed at me, because it's not
>   real Adidas.

> MUM: What is real? Is it not a real jacket? Is it
>   not keeping you warm 'for real'?

MEL sobs.

MEL: But it has two stripes instead of three,
    Mum, and that's why they were laughing.

MUM: This is why you are going to school here
    in London – so when you are grown you
    can have choice. With a good job you can
    do and buy whatever you want.

MEL: Yes, Mum.

MUM: Come, let me show you what I bought
    today:

And she's got loads of bags from where she's been shopping.
She pulls out a shoe box from one of the bags, and opens
the box!!!

It's a pair of heels – for her. She's bought herself new shoes
and she can't afford the third stripe on my jacket!?

And then she puts them on…

    MUM: You are not ready Mel!

MUM puts on the shoes.

    MUM: Look.

MUM proceeds to dance around in the new shoes.

MUM: When I was your age, I had two shoes,
    just two. One for church and one for school.
    And that school shoe was to last the whole
    school year, before my mum would even
    consider buying a new one. One year, my
    mum bought me some shoes…and when I
    say ugly, these shoes were ugly! So I went to

school and was doing all kinds of damage to this shoe so she would buy me a new one. When I came home and my mum saw the shoes damaged on my feet like that, she said she's not going to buy me a new one until the end of year, so I better find a way to fix that shoe and wear it tomorrow. I cried and I begged her, but she refused. Then I said: Mum, when I'm big I'm going to have so many shoes in every shade of every colour! And Melissa, look at me now. When Grandma flies here to visit us here she laughs – shoes everywhere. So don't mind them. You will be able to buy Adidas top to bottom when you are big, okay?

MEL: Okay, Mum.

MUM dances some more to cheer MEL up before she disappears.

TOMBOY

It's sports day, and I'm in year six. The last year of primary school. And we never had a girls' sprint or a boys' sprint, just a sprint. No track or field, just concrete. But I was going to leave my mark and take home gold. And I was fast. I'd beaten every boy when we'd practiced at play time. Every boy; except Jerome.

Now, this was our makeshift track final event:

You started with your hand on the wall and on 'GO' you hurtled full throttle to the other side of the playground where you were met by a fence, which you were to touch, turn around and then zoom back, to cross a line marked out on the floor, but you were really just aiming to get back and touch the wall.

Jerome had this jump-kick thing that he would do at the fence, like a ninja, shaving seconds off his sprint. I couldn't do that without falling over, so I had to be ahead of him before we arrived at the fence if I was to have any chance of beating him.

KAREN: On your marks…

Karen says. We call our teachers by their first names; it's a progressive primary school.

KAREN: Get set…

And I've never felt my blood being pumped so ferociously around my veins; my whole body is beating.

KAREN: Go!

We're off. Jerome and I are neck and neck. *Not ideal but you can always make a break on the return from the fence.* As I'm telling myself this Jerome gets to the fence before me, doing his legendary kick-turn off the wall and I feel like he's done it over my head as I merely brush the fence on my U-turn.

Even more determined, I convince myself I can pull it back. Just focus, just focus on Karen. Focus on getting back to that wall. FOCUS!

And for a moment it's just me charging at this wall and no one else on the concrete, a divine experience.

When suddenly I feel this sharp surge to my head. I open my eyes and I see the sky. I can hear Karen and I don't really know what's going on.

According to witnesses, in my moment of divinity, I was actually stampeding toward the finish wall as if I could run right through it – sailing past Jerome and the floor-marked finish line and colliding into said wall.

But I beat him. I beat Jerome. I won!

After a visit to the school nurse, who cleans the wound and seals the deal with a plaster (because plasters solve everything in primary school), I'm ready to collect gold and be named the fastest in the final ever primary school assembly!

After school, I'm walking home with Jennifer and I call out:

> **MEL:** Bye Jerome! Still can't believe I beat ya!

> **JEROME:** Yeah, because you're a lesbian!

He laughs as our distance grows…and Jennifer is laughing too.

> **MEL:** Do you know what a lesbian is?

I say.

> **JENNIFER:** Yeah. A woman that hates men.

> *MEL tucks the medal in her jacket. Ashamed.*

When I get home, I go into our bedroom and my big sister Alexa is getting ready to go out. I slowly remove my jacket to reveal the glorious golden pendulum swinging from my neck… And she sees it. I know Alexa sees it; but she doesn't say anything because she can't have me enjoy this moment.

> **MEL:** Alexa, am I a lesbian?

I say, getting her attention.

She laughs, comes up to me and looks at my medal; then at me.

ALEXA: Maybe, tomboy.

And she leaves.

ALEXA AND PERIODS

I've always looked up to Alexa. She's four years older than me. I remember one time she had a fringe weaved in, and I thought it was real and got scissors and cut an abomination into my own head. I was convinced it looked the same.

But Alexa just knows everything. She has *Teen Vogue*, *Elle Magazine*, she even reads the *Cosmopolitan*; so she knows all about what happens when you're a woman.

> **ALEXA:** When you're a woman every month you bleed. It's called your period.
>
> **MEL:** What makes it happen? Are you hurt?
>
> **ALEXA:** Well, apparently Andrea had hers for the first time two weeks ago. She was lucky because it happened when she was in the toilet. But then the blood wouldn't stop coming and she got scared. We all saw Miss Parson running across the playground with a bucket. When she walked in the toilet she slipped because the floor was covered. Then she made Andrea sit on the bucket and Andrea was crying so loud we could all hear her outside the toilet. When Andrea stopped Miss Parson poured all the blood down the toilet. And Andrea had to wear a pad for the next few days to absorb it all. She's got two weeks until it starts again. And there will be no warning. It just starts.

MEL is petrified.

> **MEL:** Alexa, I'm ten, you think I'm going to
> believe that?

> **ALEXA:** You'll see when it happens to you…

MEL goes to get a bucket.

I don't believe her but I'm going to carry a bucket around
just in case.

PRAYER THERAPY

Right, well, looking back there was nothing massively
wrong. So no one really explained a period… So I had a
pervy uncle; who doesn't…? And maybe my career as an
athlete has been stifled – who knows?

But none of that is huge. None of that explains why I feel
like shit. Sorry, it's just:

Look, I was raised on this: this whole Christian thing. It's
why I'm looking to you for answers. I even read your book
once. Yeah, *all* of it!

Some of it is beautifully poetic. Some of it is super epic!
Some of it is real boring…no offense.

Well, some offense – you're God, you can do better.

Alright, I digress. I haven't prayed in a while and I don't
really believe in singing the songs anymore. And it's quite
apparent I'm losing the plot.

But I just don't get it, where is my peace?!

I started secondary school three weeks ago. It's cool, because Alexa is in year eleven, so she'll help me out every now and again. What's even better is that my best friend Jennifer and I got into the same school.

Miss Morris says we'll be having a class on sex education tomorrow; and all the boys are being silly, giggling and drawing penises on the steamy windows.

I'm mature. I know about sex. I know that you have to be careful, you do it with someone you love, and I've seen a picture of a penis. They're actually really ugly.

She steams her bedroom window with her breath and begins to draw a penis. She laughs.

> **MUM:** What is that you are doing? Is that a
> penis with two balls?

> **MEL:** I'm only joking... I'm sorry Mum.
> Everyone was doing it at school...

> **MUM:** So if everyone at school is jumping off a
> cliff you will also jump, eh?

> **MEL:** No.

> **MUM:** Sit down.

MEL sits down.

And there is an endless silence... My mum looking pensive out the window. I'm not sure if she's about to end my life. The penis fades.

> **MEL:** We don't have to talk about sex. I know
> it's not for my age group.

I say, in the most mature voice I can muster.

> **MUM:** Melissa. How do you explain the colour red to a blind person?

> **MEL:** Err… It's like orange or pink, but hotter.

> **MUM:** No, they are blind. They have never seen the colour orange or pink.

> **MEL:** Oh…err. I don't know.

> **MUM:** Exactly. I don't know how to explain sex to you.

Yeah, *this* was the sex chat with my mum!

> **MUM:** When I was growing up, nobody would talk about things. We couldn't talk about these things with our parents. They used to say to us, 'Anybody who has sex early – they are dead.' That's what they told us. And that's what we believed. So you are even lucky I am having this conversation with you.
>
> I want you to get what I did not get. One man; who loves God and loves you.
>
> The Bible says, 'A man will leave his father and mother and be united to his wife, and the two will become one flesh.'
>
> So just keep yourself virgin till you marry. Because the more people go around the more they'll be polluting themselves. Don't be like this generation. Because this generation is like a car without brakes. God is missing.

But God is not missing from my life. I love being in church.

Church is somewhere where… It's like home; for your spirit, you know. We start with praise and worship:

A syncopated melody
Of voices as everyone rejoices
Creating a vigorous sense of harmony

Today Pastor Sarah is preaching about Purpose.

> **PASTOR SARAH:** 'Work out your salvation to fulfil God's good purpose.' There's great joy in the discovery of His purpose when we trust in the revealing power of being in His presence.

And I'm liberated in feeling part of something greater than myself. That as long as I trust God, he will make all things work for my good.

As I'm listening the word of God just fills my soul. It's like I lose control.

It's an unrivalled release.

More profound than words. A paramount peace.

After church, my mum comes to find us. And I want to tell her how much I was listening; how much I want to know God's purpose for my life. But before I do she says…

> **MUM:** Where is Alexa?

I didn't even notice her sneak out today.

MEL: She had to rush home because she has to
    finish her coursework.

MUM: So, you are lying now?

MEL: No her deadline is tomorrow.

MUM: Hmm. And you as well, were you
    listening today?

MEL: Yeah. My purpose is to be a model of
    Christ and a representation of his love.

FOUR-INCH PHOEBE

Phoebe is ahead of everyone at school. She's given handjobs,
blowjobs; been fingered by three different guys – one of
them isn't even in our school!! She has no shame; in fact
she's loud and proud – telling us about the second guy she's
slept with.

> **PHOEBE:** He was actually so gentle. You look
>   at him and you think he's gonna be so
>   hardcore. But he was so nice.

I wouldn't say we're friends. We're not. I'm just here because
Jennifer is. And you know Jennifer, we've been friends for
ages. She's come to church with me a few times.

They all know I'm waiting till marriage so they don't include
me. Well, Jennifer likes to tease me. She thinks I'm hornier
than anyone... I'm not.

And Phoebe's still going.

> **PHOEBE:** Like I actually felt special. He wasn't
>   in a rush, you know. Like taking his time
>   when he took off my bra. And afterwards,

you know what he said to me…? He said
your pussy is so nice because you've got a
four-inch clitoris.

MEL: What?!

PHOEBE: Look, go like this.

PHOEBE touches the tip of her index finger with that of her middle finger, creating a little gap between the two.

PHOEBE: Push as hard as you can and if you
measure from here to here… That's how
you know…

MEL is following the instructions.

PHOEBE: Oh my God Mel, you're tight. Your
first time is really going to hurt. If you ever
have a first time.

And they all laugh. Jennifer's laughing too.

I'm not worried. My first time will be magical with someone
I really love and I won't be dirty like Phoebe from all the
guys I've slept with. So I just walk away.

MICHAEL

I'm in church on Sunday, praying for Jennifer. Because
I think she just needs a little guidance to find Christ. She
just needs to come when it's Youth Take Over, like today.
One Sunday a month the Youth lead the main service and
Michael leads praise and worship. And Michael's voice
is just…

24

It's a real gift from God. He looks so pure when he takes the mic – like he's really filled with the Holy Spirit. And it's beautiful to watch.

After service, I go up to Michael, and it's weird; I feel star-struck. But it's Michael – like Michael who thought he could pull off dreadlocks with his braces. I've known him for ages. So I say:

> **MEL:** Praise and worship was on another level today.

> **MICHAEL:** Yeah, God really came down. His presence was so real. I mean this week I've really invested time in reading his word.

> **MEL:** Oh what you been reading?

> **MICHAEL:** The book of John; chapter one and verse one: 'In the beginning was the word and the word was with God and the word was God'. And I had a revelation: God is synonymous to his word. If I just read his word, he will reveal himself to me.

> **MEL:** Wow, Michael, that's so deep.

> **MICHAEL:** Yeah I know.

And he continues and I'm listening to him. It's proper cool.

> **MUM:** What is going on, between you and that boy…? The one who leads the youth choir?

> **MEL:** Michael?

> **MUM:** Ehen; Michael.

> **MEL:** Nothing. Why?

MUM: You think people cannot see you two?
  I don't want you hanging around with
  that boy.

MEL: What's wrong with him?

MUM: Just because people are in church, it does
  not mean they are in Christ. You are going
  to church to seek God, not boys. Focus on
  God, when the time is right the Lord will
  bring the right man to you.

What's she talking about? Nothing is 'going on'. Like I don't like him – we're cool, he gets me, you know. Why has she always got to ruin everything?

But the next week, when service is back to normal, I can't focus – it's like I've always got to know where Michael is (three rows in front of me and to the left). And when he leaves to go to the toilet I notice. And I want him to see me: to clock me too. But like; what does this mean?

And I'm also thinking: How does God *bring someone* to you? How do you know when it's 'the one'?

Maybe this is it? I just feel like… I dunno. I shouldn't be feeling like this.

Okay God, if Michael is the one, now what do I do?

I don't even know who to tell. I wanted to tell Jennifer but she's just gonna go on and on about sex. And I don't even want that from him; I just want to… I dunno; chill with him!!

WITH CHILD

MUM: Melissa, Alexa is pregnant.

Beat.

    MEL: Oh... Oh right

    MUM: That's all you have to say?

    MEL: Well, what did you say?

    MUM: I just said...

The word 'just' is deceiving here. She's about to give the full
recount twice over with embellishments.

    MUM: I just said; if she needs me to do anything
        to help her then I will.

And by 'anything', my mum means nothing. There's a
shame Alexa has brought to us. Pregnant out of wedlock,
at eighteen. They near-hated each other, but the Christian
thing to do is say you'll help; whether your actions will live
up to that is another question.

And just as I am going upstairs, thinking I have escaped one
of her lectures, she says:

    MUM: I hope she is having a boy. And you as
        well, if you ever decide to have children,
        have boys, they just give you less headache.

    MEL: Huh?

I say.

    MUM: ...oh, I thank God for your life eh. When
        I look at you I just give Him glory, but it
        has not been easy. And the truth is, you are
        more likely to stay married if you have boys.

I'd actually read that myself in the *Cosmopolitan*...
Apparently it's a fact.

> **MUM:** I keep saying, I want you to get what I
> did not get. This curse that is against the holy
> union of marriage in our family has to break.

And she leaves.

But what I'm really thinking is – why Alexa was telling
everyone? Soon the whole church will know and then she
won't be able to get rid...everyone would be expecting a
baby. And I know abortion is wrong. But God forgives.
No one would know, and then there wouldn't be this
disgrace. I'm ashamed for her...of her.

PREGNANCY GOSSIP

> **PHOEBE:** I hear your sister is pregnant?

Not just in church, the news was spreading around school
too; and Phoebe loves getting in everyone's business.

> **PHOEBE:** Little miss perfect and your sister's
> been banging and got herself knocked up,
> right Mel?

Everyone is looking at me, seeing if I have the balls to reply
to Phoebe. Deny or confirm what she's just said.

> **PHOEBE:** You know her life is fucked now.
> Is the guy even going to stick around?
> Didn't she know where to get the morning
> after pill?

And I'm so ashamed, I want to die. I know better than to
deny it. Everyone knows it's true. Even if it wasn't, the fact

that Phoebe has said it makes it true. Like how we now
all want to have four-inch clits. So I get on my high horse,
because I'm comfortable there.

> **MEL:** Alexa is her own person. She makes
> her own decisions. She has nothing to do
> with me!

This comeback means more to me than anyone else. I'm
denying Alexa. I hate Phoebe for comparing us. I hate
Alexa. I'm scared to become her.

PRAYER THERAPY

God, I actually thought Alexa would go to hell for that.

I separated myself
I cut her off

What the fuck was I thinking?

Whatever you fear you feed; what you feed grows and you
just become what you fear. And maybe these are my first
world problems or the tragedy of the quarter-life crisis. But
that doesn't mean you don't listen…? It doesn't mean I don't
get answers.

Honestly I feel betrayed by you
Why set up this deception?

I did everything right
I was obedient

I followed Mum when she dragged us to church. I stopped
talking to Michael; perfect Michael! Who is a dentist right
now. A dentist! And they get paid way more than doctors.

(Yes, we value our smiles over lives.) But the point is I could have had a cushty life right now with Michael.

I mean, I was seeking to understand you myself. I wanted this dream
I wanted to *'know God'*
To be a vessel that he might use to minister to his people
And now I don't know how to move forward with or without you

When I first discovered you
Your love
It was incredible
And I committed one hundred percent
I bought into it completely

And it worked for me…because I was good.

But it didn't work for Alexa; she was slipping away and I let her go because I was so fucking holier-than-thou.

I just need to hear you
I don't want a fucking sign
I want an explanation!

SPICY SEX

I basically spend the rest of my teens proving to… God. Mum. Someone. I don't know – that I'm not Alexa. That I'm going to do things right.

And when it comes to uni I get away. Away from Mum, away from Alexa and her toddler. I start afresh and everything is new! And I'm going to Christian Union and that's where I meet Jason.

I've been with Jason for ten months next week.

At the beginning there was an unspoken mutual understanding that we're waiting till marriage. But recently there's been this elephant in the room, and it's getting bigger and bigger the longer we wait and I just want to address it before it's too big and there's no room for me to understand my own thoughts or feelings. So I ask him:

> **MEL:** Jason, do you think we'll get married?

> **JASON:** Of course babe.

He says, as if it's ridiculous that I should even ask. So I say:

> **MEL:** Well if we're gonna get married anyway...?

And there's a light in his eyes. And right there and then, without words, we agree.

So I figure he's got condoms, lube and location covered, because he's done this before, before he came to Christ obviously. So what am I bringing to the table?

Well, the sexiest underwear I'm brave enough to purchase. And I was brave...these are crotchless; just to *spice* things up!

The next day, I'm heading over to his, feeling kind of nervous but so sexy. And when he opens the door, I literally pounce on him! Which seems to be the ultimate turn-on, and suddenly we're kissing and it's fierce – it's actually like the movies. We're navigating ourselves to his room. And I'm thinking, this is going to be some spicy sex! We're in his room and I push him on the bed like:

> **MEL:** Wait there babe.

In this sultry voice. Like, who do I think I am?!

I disappear into the bathroom with the plan to reemerge looking all sexy and arousing when I reveal my lilac lingerie set, which also matches my nail varnish (no biggie).

I leave the bathroom, lingerie-clad, and I stand in his bedroom doorway like:

She strikes a pose.

He looks at me like:

JASON: Oh my god babe; wow.

But he's still fumbling with his condom so he can't fully take me in. Epic fail.

So I draw the curtains, climb into bed next to him, not really knowing what to do to fill this awkwardness. Do I help him put it on?

So I just rub his leg. And wait.

JASON: You okay?

He says.

While I was rubbing I've developed this look of disdain as I've taken in his mismatched bedsheets and the tiny hole in his boxers. Did he even try? My lingerie matches my nail varnish, man.

MEL: Yeah babe, I'm good.

Then I start to kiss him on his neck and continue rubbing his leg until his condom is on, he's squeezed some lube onto his hand and is rubbing his dick.

He rolls over onto me and attempts to penetrate. And I feel this cold sensation, I'm guessing that's the lube.

This is natural, Mel. Your instinct will kick in. Just relax.

JASON: You okay?

MEL: Yeah babe, I'm good.

It's not really working. So he fingers me for a while. Which is uncomfortable. He should have cut his fingernails.

Eventually he fully penetrates. He's trying to be gentle.

JASON: You okay?

MEL: Yeah babe, I'm good. Stop asking if I'm
okay... You're spoiling the mood.

So he thrusts in silence. And it's strange; uncomfortable, like maybe a little painful...but then kind of nice. I dunno, it's weird. I'm also thinking, how do you know when it's finished? How does the climax happen? What do I need to do to get there...?

As these thoughts are careering through my mind, Jason makes...a sound, pulls out and lies next to me...

Silence.

MEL: Was that good?

I say.

JASON: Yeah.

He sighs.

JASON: Now I know God is real...

He laughs... And I laugh. I just laugh.

Thank God I didn't wait till marriage for that!

THE BRAZILIAN

So the next day I'm on the phone to Jennifer:

> **JENNIFER:** Are you guys banging now? I told you you couldn't wait…hahaha.

And I feel ashamed.

> **JENNIFER:** So come on then, fill me in. I bet Jason is big!

> **MEL:** Well he said it was good! I don't think I came though… Is that a big deal…?

> **JENNIFER:** Nah. Now you've got the first go out the way, you can have fun. You'll get there. Did you mow the lawn before?

> **MEL:** The lawn? My mum does that, she finds it therapeutic.

> **JENNIFER:** Your lady garden. Your vag. Your pubes, you dickhead!!

> **MEL:** Woah. Why are we even friends?

> **JENNIFER:** You need me in your life, or you would still be a virgin.

> **MEL:** Kind of wish I was. That was underwhelming.

> **JENNIFER:** Well obviously, if you've got the Amazon growing between your legs. Look I bought a voucher on Wowcha, you can have it. Your first Brazilian is on me.

Why do we even call it that, do Brazilians just not grow pubic hair?

So I get a train to London, because she's booked it all the way in Tooting! I'm walking up and down the high street looking for this place when I see this door, which technically isn't even on the high street, 17A.

I'm buzzed in and head downstairs into what feels like someone's basement flat. How much was this on Wowcha?

I'm met by *Jess,* her badge says – and Jess is perfect. Bright eyes, the cutest little pixie haircut. I bet her lady garden is perfectly waxed too, and she's always had perfect sex, with no hair creating friction and getting in the way of her perfect climax. I envy the bitch as she ushers me into the room.

> **JESS:** If you remove your lower half and lie on
> the bed, I'll be back in a few moments.

And she leaves me a towel. I'm not really getting the logic here; she's going to be looking into my womb pretty soon – privacy whilst I remove my underwear seems futile.

I'm lying on the bed, bush aloft, and I start to feel chilly. So I lay the towel over my Amazon, so she's not shocked when she walks in.

When is she going to walk in?

…It smells of lavender but the room is painted orange, that's really messing with my senses. Is she ever coming back?

I think I need a wee…

We hear a knock at the door.

Too late to go now…

She comes in and folds the towel vertically, revealing one vagina lip, propping my right leg up.

JESS: Just relax. Relax your head.

She says, because I'm developing a six-pack trying to see what's going on.

JESS: Have you had a Brazilian before?

I feel like she should have asked me that at the door.

JESS: Just relax.

She repeats like some mantra.

Then she pulls out this honey, which she twists around a stick, blows before coating a fraction of my lady garden with it.

It's hot… Not boiling but on the hotter side of warm… Okay…

JESS: You're gonna feel a short sharp pain in
three, two…

MEL: Argh!

Oh this bitch thinks she's funny, she doesn't say one. Haha-HA!

JESS: You alright?

MEL: Yeah, Jess. I'm good.

I don't know how I'm going to get through this. I just wanted spicy sex.

We're about halfway. I'm doing well; I'm really proud of myself.

Again, Jess does her routine, twists the honey, and this time coating the most tender unreachable vag patch.

I'm worried, I think she's gonna take my lip clean off this time. When I look to see the hair she has removed it will literally be my vag trimmings hanging loose from the wax sheet.

And little miss perfect goes again.

Three, two...

I kick out on one like a wrestler! Getting her somewhere in the face. I look at her... I've ruined her. I've ruined little miss perfect.

I am sooooo sorry. I say, with tears welling in my eyes. I can see the wax sheet on the floor, and I'm looking at it like: *those hairs are definitely thicker than the ones on my head.* And Jess is silent. She's blinking heavily like she's trying to get her eyes to focus. Or maybe she's blind? I've blinded little miss perfect.

And she says it's fine. That if I give her a few moments she'll come back and continue.

> **MEL:** Thank you so much, Jess. But I think I'll
> just leave the rest.

And I'm desperate for a wee.

I head to the bathroom; and I'm a germophobe when it comes to foreign toilets, so I'm hovering – a skill I've managed to cultivate over the years. And I'm gushing because I was holding it in that entire time. And I have no control...I can't control my flaps. I think my hairs gave my urine guidance. So I just sit on the wet toilet seat and let my bladder empty.

Thank god these skinny jeans are black…

When I get back, I try and give my left side a trim, but it doesn't remotely resemble my right. I mean, A for effort. It's a lot tidier than it was. When Jason sees it he's beside himself.

JASON laughs.

> **JASON:** Babe, I don't care what it looks like.
> I mean it's nicer now there's no hair poking
> out the sides of your sexy panties.

He laughs. And I laugh.

And he kisses me. And we have sex.

I take pleasure in his pleasure, but I don't cum. It ends when he does.

And we end when uni does. I move back home to London, he gets a job near uni; I'm waiting tables at unsociable hours, while he's being a proper adult.

And I was really losing my grip on God. I'd been lying to myself to justify things. Jennifer was right. I was just really horny.

TRYING TO KEEP UP

I don't waitress anymore, thankfully. No offense to anyone that is a waitress – you might have dreamed of becoming a waitress. In that case – living the dream.

So what do you do for a living, Mel? That's your coinage, really. What's your soul worth? What's my contribution to society if I'm not a model of the love of Jesus Christ?

Well I nearly got a First in Graphic Design, now I work for this
up-and-coming magazine company working on their cover.

Women's magazine, naturally – because women need
guidelines to life in the form of colourful articles and
illustrations.

It's not wildly difficult.

It's basically some goddess with a banging body
Who also wishes she looked like that in real life

Sex, sex, sex; How you're doing it all wrong
Page 7; Ways to keep his erection prolonged

How to look this fucking fit
And then be offended when guys like it

Women richer than you; wearing clothes
But don't feel down beat
You can get the look on the high street

Page 9; The best anti-aging shit
Modelled by someone who's just twenty-six

Have babies before it's too late
Oh wait
It already is you see
Here's how to increase your dwindling fertility
And how to be happy
All tied up uniquely
In our bi-weekly

And I know it's trash… Another moral battlefield
But if this takes off I could be set for life

I know it's trash
But I still try and keep up, and I just about am

But the standard is so fucking, man

Like these Instagram bitches
Are sexy as fuck
I look at my phone and I'm literally star-struck
Like how do you look that hot?
#NoFilter

There's just so much clickbait commotion
Constant self-promotion
And I feel like I'm losing my mind with all the *look at me*
white noise!

My mum was recently in Ghana
She told me about the mango tree. You know, the one at my
Grandma's
I just have memories
Of it providing these unrivalled mangos
She told me that it doesn't bear fruit anymore. It's just old now

And you know what I thought?
I thought, what happens when I'm old and no longer
sexy, or even sexualized? Maybe that's when you become
invisible
Completely unrecognised
I'm not even trying to provoke
But
Sexy is currency
And I'm scared to go broke

AUNTY MARGARET AND THE SPECIAL SPOT

It's my twenty-fourth birthday and my mum says:

> **MUM:** Happy birthday darling. I want to bless
> you. Amen?

MEL: Amen.

MEL goes to leave.

> **MUM:** And, wait! I also want to talk to you…
> By your age, people normally sort
> themselves out.

My mum has a knack for talking in riddles.

> **MEL:** By 'sort yourself out' do you mean…find
> somewhere to live? Are you kicking me out?

> **MUM:** No.

> **MEL:** So?

> **MUM:** So I'm saying… By your age…people
> are getting their lives in order…

Ohh! What she's saying is my life needs validating and that
can only be achieved by the partnership of an alpha male.
Alright mum… I'll just go and find one.

> **MUM:** In *Coming to America*, by twenty-one,
> Eddie Murphy was married! But you, you
> are sitting here waiting for…?

> **MEL:** Mum, young people are eighteen to
> thirty, so I've still got time…

> **MUM:** Time for what?

> **MEL:** Well… My adult life to fall into place…

> **MUM:** You are expecting your life to 'fall'? Oh
> Melissa. Fall from where? Is it manna from
> heaven? I'm praying for you every day, but

remember the Lord helps those who help
themselves, oh.

What kind of miracle is she expecting here? My whole life
it's like, God this, God that, no boys, no fun, and now she's
looking at me all disappointed! You created this mate!!

Then the phone rings.

> **MUM:** Ehen, how are you?

It is Aunty Margaret.

> **MUM:** Eh she's fine, she's here.

MEL takes the phone off MUM.

> **MEL:** Hello Aunty Margaret. Yeah it's today.
> Thank you.

And then Aunty Margaret says:

> **AUNTY MARGARET:** So, Melissa, do you have
> boyfriend?

> **MUM:** No she does not.

My mum interjects.

> **AUNTY MARGARET:** Oh Melissa, fine girl like
> dis and there's no man to appreciate…

> **MUM:** I know. You just leave her. She said she's
> waiting for her life to fall…

> **AUNTY MARGARET:** Ah! Your mum is loud.
> Go into the corridor, I want to ask you
> something.

> **MEL:** …Okay.

MEL moves.

AUNTY MARGARET: Melissa, are you a virgin?

MEL: Err…

AUNTY MARGARET: Don't worry, I won't tell your mum.

MEL: Of course I am. I'm saving myself till marriage…

AUNTY MARGARET: Is that so? Listen to me. Me, I saved myself for your uncle. And don't worry, now things are good in the bedroom. But they were not always good.

MEL: Aunty where is this coming from?!

AUNTY MARGARET: Quiet.

I'm giving you golden nuggets here.

I had to teach your uncle. When the wedding night came, I thought: Wow, I have made it; I'm a good Christian. Then I thought: Where is the chorus of angels? Where is the shining light from heaven? It was nowhere to be seen, oh! Nobody applauded my righteousness.

And when we finished that first session, I was looking to the Lord and asking him: Are you serious? I saved myself or this? I was even thinking to leave your uncle that very night! But I had to teach him.

So you better make sure you know what you like. Because the men don't know what they are doing.

MEL: Okay, thanks for the chat.

AUNTY MARGARET: Wait. Listen to me. There is a special spot. A special spot… The men don't know. They just find the entrance and will be pumping anyhow… Go and collect a mirror and look for yourself.

MEL: Oh. Wow, wow!

MUM: What? What is the matter?

MEL: Nothing, nothing. Here's the phone. She needs to talk to you…

AUNTY MARGARET: *(Echo.)* A special spot.

FIRST CUM FUN

Maybe this whole climax thing *is* me? Maybe I'm just not sexually exciting, or experienced enough to know how to get there, or what it even feels like when it's coming. But I'm still entitled to one, right?

Watch some porn! Everybody wanks watching porn. Just watch some porn – easy.

So I'm watching the first ten seconds of a few videos, and I can't settle on one. I don't know what it is… There's no love – just people smashing.

Let's try Google:

She types:

'How to make yourself climax'

She reads.

'Learn how to have intense orgasms, whether they are clitoral or vaginal…'

There are two types?

And there's loads of information from researchers, doctors, and men that have had enough sex they can educate women on their bodies.

'Start by caressing your body and when you're ready to take it to the next level, move your hands down. You'll know when you're stimulated because your clitoris will be erect; kind of like a tiny mini penis.' … Okay.

Oh! I bought this intense orgasmic lubricant gel. But I read that I'm not to use too much, or my finger will feel like a hotdog in a hallway.

And apparently the most sensitive part of your clit is the one o'clock position. So if you imagine a clock on your vagina, it will be the upper left corner of your clit; which is easier to access with you left hand… This is all incredibly technical.

Okay, forget all that, Mel. Just improvise…

Okay. Up and down. Slow build-up… Understand your body… Okay.

You got this.

Improvised build-up lines. Suddenly:

Oh… This gel isn't intense, it actually just stings. I should have trusted I could get wet on my own…

No, this is happening today! Here we go. Okay. Relax! Clear
your head. Up and down your clit. Slow build-up... relax.

More improvised build-up lines. Then:

Oh no. No... It just kinda burns. I'm gonna wash my hands.
In fact... I'm just gonna have a shower.

ONE-NIGHT STAND

So I obviously just need to have more experience! I just
need to have more sex!

Well, it's my birthday party, the perfect excuse to have a
one-night stand. I'm not massive on birthdays, just means
I didn't die. But I just thought fuck it, why not? I never do
anything. And it's easier to get laid on your birthday, right?

So I tidy up my lady garden. Any intricate bits I go for with
scissors. I tell Jennifer my ultimate birthday present; she's
good at this stuff.

> **JENNIFER:** It's your birthday and you're single,
>   we're gonna go out and get you some dick!

I've always loved the idea of a one-night stand – being a
player: I'm gonna go out tonight and I'm gonna have sex
with a stranger!

Suddenly she's in the club, dancing. She's good!

Then I catch this guy's eye. And for a second it throws me.
Just get lost in the music, Mel. You got this. Your lady garden
is tidy, and you're looking the hottest you've ever looked
in your life!

She dances and turns around.

Then he's there in front of me.

MAN FROM THE CLUB: I hear it's your birthday.

MEL: It is!

MAN FROM THE CLUB: Can I just say you look
beautiful.

MEL: I know right?!

And we dance and dance, and he gets closer and he smells
so good; just of potential sex... Potential spicy sex. He's so
close. And we kiss.

We stop.

I look at him.

And we kiss again; I feel like I'm kissing his face off. I'm so
excited! Where is this coming from?!

Then we stop.

MAN FROM THE CLUB: You want another drink?

MEL: No, I'm good. Let's go back to yours!

I just said that out loud!

Yes girl, it's about to go down!

And it's better than Jason. A lot better. I don't know why,
it's just fierce, like there's no pressure, no thoughts, it's just
animal! I don't know him, he doesn't know me, or that he's
only the second guy to be inside me. And I feel like this is
it. I'm in this stranger's house having the sex of my life. It's
definitely going to happen with this devil on the dance floor.
I'm going to climax and this is the best birthday ever!!!!!

I think I nearly got there… I think so. Well, I felt the beginning of something happening, you know.

Anyway we meet again and go for drinks; me and Mr One-Night-Stand Man… And he just talks about himself the whole time. I sit. I listen. I laugh… I listen. I laugh.

I should have just left it as a one-night stand. The magic of the night.

PRAYER THERAPY

God, I wanted to be righteous. I wanted it for Mum.
I wanted it for you. Tragic.
I was so holier-than-thou; I let my relationship with Alexa just die
Now I'm just as much a sinner as she is, but without a seven-year-old child in my stead

Jesus! What is this?
Are we cursed? What do I have to do to break it?
What did I ever do wrong?

You go on and on about love
God is Love
Love is above all things
Well none of this feels like love

I need faith
I think I'll collapse without it I don't want to walk away –
But where are you??!

You're a fraud.
And I am for believing in you; for indulging these ideas.
You're just as fucked up as we are.

All these bullshit rules. All these lies about love. It's all just
to control. To manipulate
My foundation is completely rocked.

I don't believe in anything anymore. I don't believe love is
even real.

We just mistake it for that initial primitive chemical reaction
that occurs when you're sexually attracted to someone and
then we drag that out for as long as possible...

God is love? Well love isn't real. You're a fucking fraud.
And I'm done.

SEXING STRANGERS

Now this shit is easy.

On my phone I type and I type and I type
'Nothing serious' 'Let's meet up for a drink – love meeting new
people blah blah blah...' All the euphemisms for 'just casual
fucking please'
Endless dates, laughing, just laughing at the bad jokes
All for the D
Because I'm young, single and free

And I'm completely – lost in the hype

I delete the apps...
I download them again, I swipe and swipe and swipe.
Because I'm a millennial monster
Feeding on pixels, bytes and likes
Desperately trying to keep my head above the ever-
expanding dot-com ocean
And I can't open up

Because I'm scared I'll be discarded the way I swipe any guy
to the left, just to make myself feel good
So much at my fingertips
I'm paralysed by abundance
I can't commit to anything
If you don't laugh, you cry.
I'm done laughing and I think I'm on the verge of a
monsoon of tears

It's funny how I used to think it sacred, you know. That all
I wanted was to have it with one person, have their 'spawn'
and live the perfect life

Now I feel like whoever I'm seeing at thirty-five, they will
be the lucky man whose offspring I shall bring forth.
Not everyone meets the love of their lives. I think I'm okay
with that…

UNFOLDING

MUM: Mel… Melissa?

MEL: Yes?

MUM: I'm going to church.

MEL: Okay.

MUM: Get up, I'm waiting for you to follow
me. Melissa, I'm waiting for you to get up.
Mel…?! I'm not going to ask you again.
What is wrong with you? Why are you
behaving like this!?

And I want to say:

Because I don't think it makes sense anymore

I don't even know how it did before

I want to say:

Mum, God loves us unconditionally, but we can only go to
heaven on the condition that we commit our lives to him…?

It is not good for man to be alone, I will create for him a helper,
is what we're taught
So God created Man, and Women were what, an afterthought?

Why should I adhere to this male-orchestrated form of
dominance? All of 'God's word' discredits female competence
Other than to increase the populace

This 'weaker vessel' just gets fucked
That's the biology of our autonomy
And to bring forth more fuckers, it's agony

And this faith runs intrinsically
I mean we get married in white dresses
To exhibit virginity
Our monarchy is ordained by God himself
Our calendar will forever recognize the birth and death of
our messiah

I'm just trying to decipher
This construct of control: this God you so desperately want
me to proclaim
When we were enslaved and colonized in his name

I want to say, Mum, where is that woman who looked so
fucking sexy in her sexy new shoes? But I just say:

> MEL: How can you go to church and pretend
> things are okay? You haven't seen Alexa
> in ages.

> **MUM:** Don't start, Mel! Don't start this
> nonsense. Alexa left. Alexa left us. She
> made choices…

And she's tearing up. And this is the moment. The moment I simply see…my mother's mortality.

She doesn't go to church today. She just sits downstairs, praying for me. Praying and crying. God isn't listening.

I leave. I can't be around her.

I want to see Alexa. I need to apologise. I'm her. I'm worse. So I arrive unannounced.

MEETING ALEXA

> **ALEXA:** Err, what are you doing here?

She says on the intercom.

> **MEL:** Can you let me in please?

Silence.

> **MEL:** I didn't bring a Bible.

We hear the buzzer. MEL enters.

Her door is open when I get to it. We sit. She offers me juice.

> **ALEXA:** How are you?

She says.

> **MEL:** I'm good.
>
> **ALEXA:** How's Mum?
>
> **MEL:** Fine. How's Malachi?

ALEXA: He's fine. He's so bright.

And she points to a marked spelling test on the fridge. Ten out of ten. I feel like the word 'miscommunication' is a bit difficult for an eight-year-old…but he got it right…!

ALEXA: So, how's God?

She laughs.

And I just cry.

> MEL: He's disappointed, man… I've been
> shagging so many strangers. I just thought
> if I'm cursed I might as well go all out! I've
> been chasing the dick. Sometimes pussy too.
> I'm definitely going to hell.

ALEXA: Live your life, Mel! Does Mum know?

> MEL: No. Maybe. I don't know. I need to move
> out. I hate her. I'm a fucking mess, man.

> ALEXA: Oh my God, Mel. Live your life. You're
> twenty-five; if you make mistakes, you make
> mistakes. Mum was just doing her best. I
> can tell you it's not easy, you know.

Suddenly I feel like I'm nine again. Wanting to cut a fringe in my hair to be cool like her. She's incredible.

> ALEXA: Mel, your body is yours, you can fuck
> who you want.

MEL: I don't know… I don't know.

> ALEXA: It's okay not to know. People will
> always have shit to say…but you've got to
> trust yourself.

Beat.

> **MEL:** When did you become so nice…?

> **ALEXA:** When I decided to forgive you. And
>   maybe that was God, however he, she, it
>   exists… But I had to heal first.

Beat.

> **MEL:** What time do you have to pick up Malachi?

> **ALEXA:** Mel, you can't just walk into his life
>   like that.

GIRL IN THE HOT PANTS

I'm on the tube, on the way home; and there's this girl with
her dad, opposite me. She's wearing these denim hot pants
and she's so energetic.

> **GIRL:** Daddy, how many stops? Embankment,
>   Charing Cross, Piccadilly Circus and then
>   Oxford Circus. What happens if we go all
>   the way to Harrow and Wealdstone, Dad?

I'm sitting there watching this girl like: *Sit down and close your
legs.* I would've known not to behave like that. Maybe it's
because she's around her dad, and if she was with her mum,
her mum would be on it. She's about ten… Old enough to
know.

And then I caught myself. Why did I have that expectation
of her?

Maybe part of me envied that untamed energy, and how she
didn't have a self-awareness, a responsibility for how open
she was with her body.

And then I thought, I hope she never loses that energy…
I hope it's never tamed.

THE END

9 781786 828538